D0516407

The Dreamtime

AUSTRALIAN ABORIGINAL MYTHS

Also by Ainslie Roberts and Charles P. Mountford
THE DAWN OF TIME

THE DREAMTIME

AUSTRALIAN ABORIGINAL MYTHS
IN PAINTINGS BY **AINSLIE ROBERTS**
WITH TEXT BY **CHARLES P. MOUNTFORD**

Line Illustrations by Ainslie Roberts

RIGBY LIMITED

RIGBY LIMITED, ADELAIDE • SYDNEY
MELBOURNE • BRISBANE • PERTH
FIRST PUBLISHED 1965
REPRINTED SEPTEMBER 1966
REPRINTED APRIL 1967
REPRINTED FEBRUARY 1968
REPRINTED JULY 1969
REVISED IN FULL COLOUR MARCH 1970
REPRINTED OCTOBER 1971
COPYRIGHT © 1965 AINSLIE ROBERTS AND CHARLES P. MOUNTFORD
LIBRARY OF CONGRESS CATALOG CARD NUMBER 65-23900
NATIONAL LIBRARY OF AUSTRALIA CARD NUMBER & ISBN 0 85179 025 9
ALL RIGHTS RESERVED
WHOLLY SET UP AND DESIGNED IN AUSTRALIA
PRINTED BY TOPPAN PRINTING CO. (H.K.) LTD, HONG KONG

TO THE BROWN PEOPLE
who handed down these Dreamtime Myths

CONTENTS

THE
DREAMTIME

AUSTRALIA IS AN ANCIENT LAND, UNDISTURBED BY ANY
major geological upheavals for many millions of years. Its people, too,
are an ancient people, who, reaching the shores of this continent fifteen
thousand or more years ago, were able to follow their simple way of
life until we, the white intruders, came among them.

No other race has ever lived in Australia, nor at the present time are
there people of the same stock anywhere else in the world, except,
perhaps, the pre-Dravidians of India, and the almost extinct Veddahs
of Ceylon, who may be distantly related.

There is no evidence that the Australian natives originated in their
present homeland; but, wherever they came from, it is reasonable to
assume that they left south-eastern Asia and travelled to Australia
through the Indonesian and Melanesian Islands, their journey spanning
probably many hundreds of years.

Although Cape York, on the north-eastern corner of the continent,
would have been the easiest and most reasonable point of entry, some
groups may have landed along the north-western coasts of the continent.
Irrespective, however, of their points of entry, these brown-skinned
people were living in every part of Australia—from the fertile, well-
watered coastal regions, to the arid, inhospitable interior—many
thousands of years before European settlement reached their homeland.

It is certain that the aborigines have always been, as they are today, simple hunters and food-gatherers, collecting their sustenance at such time and place as Nature provided. In seasons of plenty they feasted, and in times of hardship they philosophically endured hunger, confident that some foods would soon be ready for harvesting.

The equipment of the aborigines is particularly limited. Except along the coastline, or on the larger rivers, where fishing is an activity, the men own little more than spears, spearthrowers, boomerangs, and clubs; and the women use wooden, bark, or string containers, grinding-stones to reduce grass-seeds into a coarse flour, and simple digging-sticks for unearthing tubers and small creatures.

Some tribes use simple watercraft, but over the vast stretches of the Australian coastline the aborigines are without any means of travelling by water. They do not know how to weave cloth to cover themselves, have no pottery techniques by which to make cooking vessels, nor any beasts of burden on which to travel or carry goods. From the standpoint of material possessions the aborigines of Australia are, without doubt, the poorest of any people.

This material poverty has led to the mistaken impression that, as the white man uses so many, and the aborigines so few tools with which to gain a livelihood, the aborigines must have the lesser intelligence. But this idea is completely refuted on an examination of the success of the food-gathering of the aborigines in the almost waterless deserts of central Australia, a country so arid that no white man can live there unless he takes his own food.

Yet, with no more than five tools, the aborigines have been able to live and multiply in this harsh and unfriendly country for many centuries. This is surely evidence not only of normal intelligence, but of minds intensely trained in the lore of the desert, and in the knowledge of its food resources.

The aborigines live in family groups, each group having its own territory, which its members seldom leave, except to attend some important ceremony, or when there is a shortage of food or water. All members of the family, from children to the oldest men and women, engage in a continuous search for food, a search that must go on from day to day, for they have no means of storing or preserving what they kill or collect.

To meet these conditions, the natives must acquire a profound knowledge of the rhythm of their country. From early years they learn when the vegetable foods ripen, and where they may be gathered; the seasons of the year when the reptiles wake from their winter sleep, when the animals reproduce, and in what place there will be water to drink.

The aborigines have also developed a calendar, based on the movements of the heavenly bodies, the flowering of certain trees and grasses, the mating calls of the local birds, and the arrival of migrant ones. All these signs are related to the food-cycles on which their living depends.

The labour of food-gathering is fairly equally divided between the men and the women. To catch the larger creatures—the kangaroos, the wallabies, and the emus—the men often have to make long journeys in the cold of winter or the blazing heat of summer. The women, laden with the children and the camp gear, travel in a more or less straight line from one stopping place to the next, gathering vegetable foods, fruits, and small creatures on the way. The men often return empty-handed at the end of the day, for the desert animals are wary and difficult to capture, but the women always bring in some food. Sometimes it is not much, nor particularly tasty, but it is usually enough to keep the family going until the hunters are more successful.

The distribution of the food is governed by wise laws, decreeing that everyone receives a share, whether the amount be large or small, or the recipients men, women, or children. Further, though meat is highly prized, the hunter gains little advantage from his prowess. The hunter's share is the lesser portion; his skill is of more value to his family than to him. His reward is in the joy of achievement and the approbation of his fellows.

It is a memorable experience to live and travel with these aboriginal people, and to observe, if only for a short time, the functioning of one of the most primitive cultures of mankind, a culture where the gaining of a livelihood is a remarkable achievement; where the people live in harmony with each other and their surroundings, and the laws are well balanced and strictly enforced.

The government of these people is in the hands of the well-informed old men, not the physically active youths. A full knowledge of the secret and ceremonial life of the tribe is possessed only by these elders. It is they who maintain the ancient laws, agree on the punishments of the law-breakers, and decide when the rituals, on which the social and philosophical life of the tribe depends, will be performed. It is not, therefore, the task of a professional or priestly class to preserve the traditional myths and their associated rituals, but of a number of groups of fully initiated men, each group being responsible for the memorizing of the myths, songs, and rites belonging to their family territories, and for the passing of them on, unaltered, to the succeeding generation.

The organization of each tribe, in its basic form, is divided into two intermarrying groups; for example, one half are the Crow people, and the other the Eaglehawk people. It is a fundamental law that a man must always marry outside of his group, and the same applies to women. An Eagle-man must marry a Crow-woman, or vice versa. To marry a member of the same class would be looked on much the same as marrying a brother or a sister, and punishable by death.

The aborigines believe that their world is flat, and so limited in area that, should they travel to the horizon, which to them is the edge of the universe, they would be in danger of falling into bottomless space. Most tribes assume that the world has two levels; the earth, which is the home of the aboriginal men and women, and the sky, in which the sun, moon, and star people live, as well as, during the dry season, the rainstorms, the thunder, and the lightning.

According to some tribes, the home of the dead—that is, the aboriginal "heaven"—is also in the sky, although other aboriginal groups consider that, when dead, they will take their eternal rest on a distant island, in a dense jungle, or in some other inaccessible place.

At the conclusion of the burial rituals, which often extend over several months, the spirit of the dead person, leaving its burial place, sets out on a journey to its future home. Sometimes the spirit is ferried to its destination by a ghostly boatman, sometimes it is guided by a bird of the night, and sometimes it is met by a party of spirits who have been waiting for their old friend to join them. In the "heaven" of the aborigines there is an abundance of food, good weather, comfortable camping places, and a community of old friends, all of whom are at peace with each other.

The aborigines, not aware of the facts of physical paternity, believe in the existence of tiny, self-supporting spirit children who are always on the look-out for earthly mothers. The homes of these spirit children are in many places: above the blue vault of the sky, which, to the aborigines, is little higher than the tallest tree, in rocky clefts, in hollow trees, or in waterholes. When a little spirit, peering out from its hiding place, sees a woman whom it thinks will make a good mother, it enters her body and starts life as a human being.

Although the aboriginal idea of the creation of the world is much the same, in general pattern, throughout Australia, the details vary from tribe to tribe. The following myth from central Australia is typical of many:

In the beginning, before there was any life, the earth was flat and featureless, unbroken by any mountain range, watercourse, or major natural feature. Nor was it inhabited by any living thing.

Then, at some time in the long-distant past, which the aborigines poetically refer to as the "Dreamtime," giant, semi-human beings, resembling one or the other of the creatures in appearance, but behaving like men and women, rose out of the featureless plains, where they had been slumbering for countless ages, and started to wander aimlessly over the countryside. As they wandered, these Dreamtime heroes carried out the same tasks as do the aborigines of today; they camped, made fire, dug for water, fought each other, or performed ceremonies.

Then, mysteriously, this Dreamtime came to an end, and wherever these creators had been active, some mountain range, isolated hill, valley, watercourse, or other natural feature now marks the place. When the aborigines are asked what brought about this remarkable change they reply that they do not know, but feel sure that if some wise old man of an earlier generation had been present, he could have answered the question.

These people of the Dreamtime made everything with which the aborigines are in daily contact: the land on which the aborigines live, and from which they gain their living; the food creatures that live there, the first spears and spearthrowers to assist the men in capturing the larger creatures, the wooden dishes, the grinding-stones to help the women to prepare the food, and fire, both to cook that food and to keep the people warm.

The same Dreamtime heroes also decreed the laws that govern all aspects of the secular and sacred life of the tribe; the relationship of each member of the community to the other; the ceremonies that must be performed before men can be admitted more deeply into the secret rituals of the tribe; and the supernatural penalties that all will suffer who disobey these ancient laws. The myths of these ancient times are accepted as absolute truth, and an answer to all the questions of living. The saying, "As it was done in the Dreamtime, so must it be done today," has established the laws of behaviour that all must obey.

These myths also dominate the cultural life of the native people. They are the subject of their graphic arts; the inspiration of their music, and the core of their rich and extensive ceremonial life, the medium by which the tribesmen keep alive the memories of the Dreamtime heroes and the laws they made.

The myths of the Australian aborigines are comparable with those of the ancient civilizations of the world; to take but two, those of ancient Greece, whose Homeric tales describe how the gods and demi-gods of Olympia created many of the mountains, the volcanoes, and the coastline of the eastern Mediterranean; and the sagas of the Nordic races whose early gods made the complete universe—the earth, the sky, the seas, and all natural forces.

The myths of ancient Greece and Scandinavia, like those of the aborigines, did more than account for the origin of the world about them; they provided a philosophy that governed the lives of the people, and from that philosophy a force that stimulated their cultural life.

One has only to consider the incalculable influence of the myths of ancient Greece on the literature, drama, and art of the civilized world for over two thousand years, and that of the Nordic myths on the music, drama, and literature of northern Europe, to realize how the living myths of the aborigines, which belong so fully to Australia, could contribute to the cultural life of this country.

But as yet our writers, musicians, dramatists, and artists, still dominated by the influences of overseas cultures, have been but little inspired by the beauty of the mythical beliefs of our native people.

Suddenly, this rich store of beauty has been revealed to us through the paintings of Ainslie Roberts. With the creative mind of the true artist, free from all influences except those of the mythical stories of the brown-skinned aborigines, he has given us pictures as full of imagery and fantasy as the stories on which they are based, pictures that reveal both the sensitive mind of the artist and the fertile imagination of the aboriginal story-teller.

CHARLES P. MOUNTFORD

St. Peters, South Australia

BOORA THE PELICAN

In the long-distant past, Boora the Pelican, in his sleek black plumage (all pelicans were black in those days), owned a bark canoe. Boora did not really need a canoe, for he could swim from place to place just as easily as he could paddle, but it pleased him to know that he had something which the other birds did not possess.

One day, after a heavy storm had flooded the country, Boora saw, on a mud island in the middle of a turbulent river, a man and three women sitting on a stranded log. After many entreaties Boora agreed to rescue the aborigines, but, being attracted by the youngest and prettiest girl, Kantiki, he secretly planned to steal her for himself.

So, one by one the pelican ferried the aborigines across, leaving Kantiki until last. But when Boora left with his third passenger, Kantiki, terrified at his obvious intentions, took the skin rug from her shoulders and, wrapping it around a log about the same size as herself, laid it on the sodden ground and slipped quietly into the water, hoping to reach her companions on the distant bank.

When Boora, full of expectation, returned to collect his prize, he was so angry at finding the girl asleep, that he kicked the figure with all his might, severely injuring his foot. Furious over the loss of Kantiki, at the pain in his foot, and at being made to look ridiculous, he paddled back to his camp. Splashing white paint over his head and body, in the same way as the aborigines do when about to take part in a fight, Boora was on the point of setting out to recapture Kantiki when the older pelicans saw his painted body.

They were so disgusted with his appearance that, attacking Boora with their long beaks, they drove him from the camp, decreeing at the same time that pelicans must never change their colour.

Yet, in spite of this, so many of the younger birds, who tired of their sombre plumage, painted themselves with white, that today all the pelicans seen on the shores of the lakes, or feeding in the billabongs, are black and white, just as Boora was so long ago.

28″ x 38″   *Mr Rhys A. Roberts*

THE FIRST KANGAROO

One Australian myth relates how the first kangaroos were blown to the Australian mainland by a violent windstorm. The creatures became exhausted on that journey, for they could not land, even though their hind legs had grown longer and longer in their attempts to gain a foothold.

A party of aborigines were out hunting when this extraordinary storm of wind swept across their country, uprooting the trees, tearing the grass and shrubs from the earth, and driving the aborigines into the shelter of the rocks. As the hunters looked upward at the clouds of swirling debris they saw the kangaroos being carried along by the storm.

Never before had the aborigines seen such strange animals, with their small heads and small arms, large bodies and tails, and long legs with which they were always trying to touch the ground, only to be swept into the air by the next blast of wind. But during a short lull in the storm the hunters saw a kangaroo become entangled in the branches of a tree, fall to the ground, and hop away.

Knowing that so large a creature would provide food for many people, the whole tribe moved to the locality where the hunters had seen the kangaroo, for it was good country with streams of running water, much fruit on the trees, and grass on the ground.

But it was a long time before the aborigines learnt how to capture the kangaroos, the largest and swiftest of all the Australian animals.

The First Kangaroo

27" x 36"   *Rt Hon. Sir Robert G. Menzies*   19

THE SUN-WOMAN
AND THE MOON-MAN

Life was difficult for the aborigines when the world was young, for, having neither light nor heat, the people were forced to search for their food in the darkness, and having found it, had to eat it raw.

One day, Purukupali (the first man in the world) and his companion, Japara, were rubbing two sticks together just to see what would happen when, by chance, they found out the way to make fire.

Purukupali, realizing that they had discovered something that would dispel the darkness, and also give heat for the aborigines to cook their food and to keep themselves warm, gave a large torch of blazing bark to his sister, Wuriupranala, and a smaller one to his friend, Japara, telling them that whatever happened they must always keep those torches burning.

When the creation period came to an end, and the mythical people were transformed into creatures, plants, and natural forces, Wuriupranala became the Sun-woman and Japara became the Moon-man.

In the morning, when the Sun-woman rises in the east with her torch of blazing bark, the aborigines leave their camps to collect food from the jungle, plain, and sea-coast. As the sun reaches its zenith, Wuriupranala, lighting a fire to cook her food, makes the day so hot that the aborigines retire to the shade of the trees. About mid afternoon they continue their food-gathering until the Sun-woman disappears over the western horizon.

It is then that the Moon-man, Japara, with the smaller torch, makes his journey across the sky to overcome the darkness of the night.

30″ x 40″   *Mr Charles P. Mountford*

THE WEDGE-TAILED EAGLE, THE WHITE COCKATOO, AND THE BLANKET LIZARD

Yurumu the Eagle-man, his wife Narina, and his friend Kilpuruna, all lived in the same camp.

One day, when the woman was in the forest collecting food, Kilpuruna met her and asked for something to eat. She offered him an opposum, which he would not take, then many other kinds of food, until Kilpuruna admitted he was not hungry; he really wanted Narina to go into the forest with him.

At first Narina refused, saying that her husband, Yurumu, would be angry if she did this. By persistence and flattery, however, Kilpuruna finally had his way.

On returning to camp, Narina, feeling ashamed of what she had done, told her husband. Though Yurumu was angry and punished his wife, he did not mention the matter to Kilpuruna, but bided his time to take vengeance.

Later, when the two men were in a high tree searching for honey, Yurumu the Eagle-man, seeing the opening of a hive on a tall branch, asked Kilpuruna to climb up and take a closer look. Not suspecting treachery, Kilpuruna did so, and was about to examine the hive when Yurumu, pushing him from the tree, watched him crash on the ground below.

Kilpuruna, flattened out by his fall, became the blanket lizard; Narina changed herself into a white cockatoo that flies from place to place calling mournfully for Kilpuruna; Yurumu, now the wedge-tailed eagle, searches eternally to find and destroy his wife's lover, the blanket lizard.

36″ x 30″   *Mr E. Joffre Smiley*   23

YIRBAIK-BAIK AND HER DOGS

Long, long ago, when many of the animals were still human beings, there lived an old woman, Yirbaik-baik, who kept a large pack of dingoes. She had trained them since they were puppies, and they were fierce and cunning. To Yirbaik-baik the other aborigines were merely food, for she and the dingoes lived only on the flesh of human beings.

Yirbaik-baik had devised many schemes to satisfy this unnatural hunger, one of which was to roam through the bush until she met a hunting party. She would then tell them that she had seen wallabies feeding not far away, and if they waited where they were she would drive the game in their direction. With spears and boomerangs ready the aborigines would wait excitedly. But when Yirbaik-baik appeared it was with her pack of hungry dingoes, who surrounded the unfortunate people, killed them, and took their bodies back to Yirbaik-baik's camp.

After a time, the other aborigines missed such a large number of their companions. Upon finding out what had happened, they surrounded Yirbaik-baik and her dogs and killed them all. As the dingoes died, their bodies changed into tiger-snakes and slid away into the bush. The skulls of the murdered aborigines were transformed into white boulders, and Yirbaik-baik herself became a small brown bird that ran hurriedly into the bush and disappeared.

The little bird, not often seen by man, usually gives its call at night. But if, after a long dry spell, the aborigines hear its voice in the daytime, they know that it is Yirbaik-baik calling up the thunderstorms to refresh the parched earth and give water to all living creatures.

27" x 36"   *Mrs P. Daniell*

THE ORIGIN OF FIRE

Stories of the discovery of fire are common in the folk tales of all primitive peoples.

There is considerable diversity in the aboriginal myths dealing with the origin of fire. Some tribes believe that it originated in a lightning flash, others that it came from a burning mountain, or that it was accidentally discovered by man. A myth of the aboriginal people who lived on the north-western coasts of Australia tells how their fire came from the sky.

Two brothers named Kanbi and Jitabidi lived in the heavens. Their camp was near the Southern Cross, and their fires were the Pointers, Alpha and Beta Centaurus. At that time there was no other fire in the universe.

Food was getting scarce in the sky-world, so Kanbi and Jitabidi came to earth, bringing their firesticks with them. They established their camp, and laid their firesticks on the ground while they went out to hunt oppossums.

The two hunters were away so long that the firesticks, becoming bored, began to chase each other about in the grass and among the branches of the trees. This game started a bushfire that burnt out much of the surrounding country. Seeing the smoke and the flames, the brothers returned at once to their earthly camp, recaptured the playful firesticks, and restored them to their place in the sky.

It happened that a group of aboriginal hunters saw the fire and felt its warmth. Realizing the value of this strange new element, they took a blazing log back to their own camp, from which many other fires were lit. Now all aborigines have the fire that once belonged only to the men of the Southern Cross.

28″ x 48″   *Mr V. G. Pike*

GOOLAGAYA AND THE WHITE DINGO

The aborigines often tell their boys and girls the story of a spiteful woman, Goolagaya, who, having no children of her own, was intensely jealous of other women who were more fortunate.

Her tale-bearing and gossip had caused almost every quarrel in the camp, especially those between husbands and wives, or mothers and their grown-up daughters. In consequence, Goolagaya was so much shunned and disliked that her only companion was a savage white dingo, which followed its mistress everywhere. But in spite of her enmity towards grown-ups, Goolagaya was always kind to children, and often, when their parents were not watching, amused them with games, or gave them titbits of food.

One day, after a violent quarrel with a woman named Naluk, Goolagaya planned to take revenge by giving her a great fright. She waited until there was no one about, then picked up Naluk's baby, and hid it under a low shrub at the edge of a distant lagoon, expecting that the infant would soon be found. But her plans miscarried, for the baby, on waking, crawled to the bank of the lagoon, fell over the edge into the water, and was drowned.

This accident so enraged the aborigines that they killed both Goolagaya and her dingo, burying them deeply in the mud of the lagoon so that never again would they cause any trouble. But though their bodies remained under the ground, their two spirits escaped and made their home in the trunk of a misshapen tree at the edge of the water.

Every night, just as the sun is sinking below the horizon, the spirits of Goolagaya and her companion leave the tree, ready, when darkness comes, to roam the bush and steal any wandering child. But Goolagaya is seldom successful, for the children, warned of the dangers of the dark, fear to leave the light of their camp-fire.

29" x 36"   *Mrs R. W. LeMessurier*

THE DEATH OF JININI

When the world was young there was no death. This calamity was brought about by the wrongdoings of the woman Bima, and her lover Japara.

Bima had a son, Jinini, of whom her husband, Purukupali, was very fond. Every morning when Bima set out to collect food she took Jinini with her, and every evening she brought him back to his doting father, together with the food she had gathered.

An unmarried man, Japara, who lived in the same camp, constantly followed Bima and persuaded her to leave Jinini under the shade of a tree while she accompanied him into the jungle. This intrigue had been going on for some time when, on one very hot day, Bima and her lover stayed away too long. When the mother returned, she saw, to her horror, that the shade of the tree had moved and Jinini was lying dead in the blazing sun.

When the father heard of the tragedy, he was demented with rage and grief. He punished his wife severely for her carelessness, then, picking up the dead body of Jinini, Purukupali walked into the sea and drowned himself. At the same time he decreed that, as his son had died, so must the whole of creation die, never to come to life again. And so it has remained from those remote times until now.

27″ x 36″   *Brigadier W. W. Wearne*

THE MEN OF THE MILKY WAY

There is a Melville Island myth that tells how, in the long distant past, the Maludaianini people were always sneaking into the jungle with the women of other men, even though they had wives of their own. This behaviour caused a great deal of jealousy and bickering that finally developed into a fight in which some of the men were killed. After this the Maludaianini people went into the sky, the men becoming the Milky Way; the women some of the near-by stars.

When the sun-woman, Wuriupranala, disappears behind the western horizon, and the light of her torch has faded, the men of the Milky Way travel in a wide band across the sky, visiting their wives as they go.

Early in the evening the Maludaianinis rub the dried perspiration from their bodies. This, falling on the aborigines' eyelids, makes them so heavy that before long the people are asleep behind their simple bark shelters.

The next morning, just as the stars and the Milky Way are beginning to fade and the first light of the Sun-woman appears in the eastern sky, the soft melodious call of the honey-eater, Tukimbini, wakes the aborigines from their sleep for the duties of yet another day.

33

21″ x 36″   *Mr W. Royston Griffiths*

KOOBOR THE DROUGHT-MAKER

The aborigines believe that if the body of a dead Koala is not treated properly, its spirit will cause the rivers to dry up, and everyone will die of thirst. A myth from south-eastern Australia tells how this belief originated.

An orphaned Koala-boy, Koobor, was constantly ill-treated and neglected by his relatives. Although he had learnt to live on the foliage of the gum-trees, he was never given sufficient water to quench his thirst.

One morning, when his relatives set out to gather food, they forgot to hide their water-buckets, so that for once in his life Koobor had enough to drink. But, realizing that unless he stored some water for himself he would soon be thirsty again, the boy, collecting all the buckets, hung them on a low sapling. Then, climbing into the branches, he chanted a special song that caused the tree to grow so rapidly that it was soon the tallest in the forest.

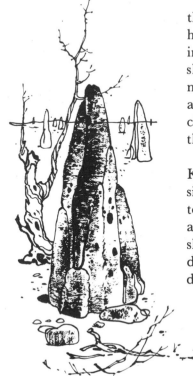

When the people returned in the evening, tired and thirsty, they were indignant to see the water-buckets hanging at the top of a very high tree, with Koobor sitting in the midst of them. The men demanded that Koobor should return the stolen water, but he replied that, as he now had all the water, it was their turn to go thirsty. After a number of attempts had been made to climb the tree, two clever medicine-men succeeded, and, harshly beating him, threw the little thief to the ground.

As the people watched, they saw the shattered body of Koobor change into a Koala, climb into a near-by tree, and sit in the top branches, where today he does not need water to keep him alive. Koobor then made a law that, though the aborigines may kill him for food, they must not remove his skin or break his bones until he is cooked. Should anyone disobey, the spirit of the dead Koala will cause such a severe drought that everyone except the Koalas will die of thirst.

36" x 48"   *Mr and Mrs David H. Brown*   35

THE BANISHMENT
OF THE CUCKOOS

This myth from eastern Australia refers to the time when the great creator Byamee began to make the earth. First he made the steep mountain ranges, the deep fern-tree gullies, the rich table lands, and the grass-covered plains. Then he created everything that moves on the surface of the earth— kangaroos, bandicoots, reptiles, and a host of smaller creatures.

Finally Byamee brought birds into the world; the birds of the bush—willy-wagtails, honey-eaters, and cuckoos; the birds of the air—eagles, crows, and swallows; and the water-birds—pelicans, ducks, and brolgas.

Byamee taught the birds how to make their nests, each in its own way; when to lay their eggs; when they were to be hatched; and how to feed the young until they were able to fly. All the birds obeyed Byamee's instructions except the cuckoos, who announced that they had no intention of building nests or of rearing their young; they only wanted to sing in the trees all day long.

The other birds, angry at the cuckoos' attitude, called a meeting to persuade them to accept their responsibilities, but in vain. Enraged by the cuckoos' selfishness, the birds rose in a body and drove them to the far north. From that time, every bird has been the enemy of the cuckoo.

When spring comes, the cuckoos fly south again to lay their eggs in the nests of other birds, leaving the hatching and feeding of their offspring to the foster-parents.

But when the young cuckoos are fully grown, they follow with unerring accuracy the path taken by their parents, without any previous knowledge or guidance, except that given to them by the great creator, Byamee.

27″ x 36″   *Mrs H. H. Harvey*

37

TIDDALIK THE FLOOD-MAKER

Tiddalik, the largest frog ever known, awoke one morning with an unquenchable thirst. He started to drink, and he drank until there was no fresh water left in the world. The creatures everywhere were soon dying and the trees were shedding their leaves because of the lack of moisture. It seemed that very soon Tiddalik the frog would be the only one alive.

The animals could not think of a way out of their terrible plight, until a wise old wombat suggested that if Tiddalik could be made to laugh, all the imprisoned water would flow out of his mouth.

So everyone gathered by the giant frog's resting-place. For a long time they tried to make him laugh, but in vain. The kookaburra told his funniest stories, so good that he could not help laughing at them himself; the kangaroo jumped over the emu; and the blanket lizard waddled up and down on two legs making his stomach protrude; but the frog's face remained blank and indifferent.

Then, when the animals were in despair, the eel, Nabunum, driven from his favourite creek by the drought, slithered up to the unresponsive frog, and began to dance. He started with slow, graceful movements, but as the dance became faster he wriggled and twisted himself into the most grotesque and comical shapes, until suddenly Tiddalik's eyes lit up and he burst out laughing. And as he laughed, the water gushed from his mouth and flowed away to replenish the lakes, the swamps, and the rivers.

The Flood-Maker

Alexis Roberts

27" x 36"   *Mrs Maurice Thiem*   39

THE STORMS OF THE
WILLY-WAGTAIL

The aborigines of southern, central, and northern Australia regard the willy-wagtail either with fear or with hostility.

In South Australia the bird is looked upon as the harbinger of death, and its presence in or around a native camp is the cause of much alarm. Along the northern coasts of the continent, although the aborigines are not actually afraid of the bird, they regard it with antipathy, knowing it to be a liar and a mischievous tell-tale. Should the women learn anything of the affairs of the men, however small the matter, it is assumed that the willy-wagtail is the culprit. In fact, the bird has such a bad reputation in these matters that the tribal elders always hunt it away before they discuss anything of ceremonial importance.

Although, according to the mythical stories of central Australia, and especially of Ayers Rock, it was a willy-wagtail woman who brought the spirit children to their aboriginal mothers, everyone regards the living bird with dread. Should an aboriginal injure or kill a willy-wagtail, the spirit of the bird, angry at such treatment, would create storms of such violence that man and the creatures would all be destroyed.

29″ x 36″   *Mr Robert H. Irwin*

41

PURUPRIKI AND THE FLYING FOXES

Before that sparkling galaxy of light, the Milky Way, spanned the heavens, there were no roads in the sky.

On earth, the aboriginal people were contented and happy. They spent the hours of daylight by collecting the abundant foods of the jungle and the seashore, and the evenings in chanting their songs and performing their ceremonies around the campfire.

The most famous singer and actor in the tribe was Purupriki, and the songs he chanted and the dances he performed were his own creation.

There came a day when the men of a neighbouring tribe paid a visit to see the performances of Purupriki. Many hours of that evening were spent in feasting, dancing, and singing, but early the next morning the men were out in the bush collecting food for the festivities of the following night.

Waiting until just before dawn, Purupriki, creeping through the darkness of the mangrove swamps, threw his club into a tree in which a myriad of flying foxes were roosting. Angry at the attack, they swept down on Purupriki and, with a roar of wings, carried him through the dim corridors of the mangrove swamps into the firmament.

On looking up, the aborigines saw Purupriki being carried into the sky by a multitude of flying foxes that trailed behind him like a luminous pathway. And as the men listened they heard the sweet voice of their much-loved singer chanting his song of farewell.

That night the tribesmen danced and chanted Purupriki's farewell song. And in the sky, looking down upon the men who did him honour, was Purupriki, now the bright star Antares, while stretching across the firmament were the flying foxes, transformed into that brilliant spectacle of the night sky, the Milky Way.

36″ x 27″   *Mr Kenneth Myer*

43

TIRLTA AND THE
FLOWERS OF BLOOD

At the time this story begins, the elders of a central
Australian tribe had decided that a young girl, Purlimil,
should be given in marriage to a coarse, jealous old man,
Tirlta. This was exceedingly bad news for Purlimil, for she
not only detested Tirlta, but she and a young man named
Borola had already planned to marry and live with his
relatives in a country far away to the east. That night,
knowing that the decision was final, the lovers eloped, and
fled to the land of his people, where they set up their camp
on the shores of a beautiful lake. There they lived happily
for so long that they had almost forgotten Tirlta.

But after several years, Tirlta, his mind still full of hatred,
assembled his relatives and attacked the people with whom
Purlimil was living. Tirlta had planned to capture Purlimil
for himself, killing everyone else in the tribe; but his
scheming was of no avail, for in the confusion of the attack
every member of the tribe was slain, including Purlimil,
the blood from their wounds staining the ground on which
they lay.

The next season Tirlta returned to gloat over the
bleached skeletons of his victims. But he saw no bones, only
carpets of scarlet flowers with black eyes that had grown
from the blood of the slain. Knowing by this that the spirits
of the dead were still active and powerful, Tirlta turned
to flee; but a spear thrown from a cloud overhead struck
him lifeless to the ground.

The tears of the spirits turned the sweet clear lake to salt,
and Tirlta and the spear that killed him are only small
stones on its shores; but every season, Sturt's desert peas, or,
as the aborigines call them, the Flowers of Blood, spread
their brilliance over the arid plains of the outback country.

27″ x 36″   *Mrs E. Stacy*

BIMA THE CURLEW

When Purukupali heard that the death of his son was caused by the conduct of his wife Bima and her lover Japara, the rage of the father was unbounded.

After striking his wife over the head with a club, and hunting her into the jungle, he attacked Japara. The two men, locked in a deadly struggle, fought for hours, each wounding the other so severely that they finally fell to the ground exhausted.

When Purukupali, recovering slightly, walked into the sea with his dead son and drowned himself a great change came over the world.

Japara became the Moon-man and rose into the sky, the wounds made by Purukupali still visible on his face. Bima, mother of the dead Jinini, was changed into a curlew who even now roams the forest at night, wailing with remorse and sorrow over the loss of her son and the calamity she brought to the world.

Blank, the Frightened Curlew.

A McKie Robinson
1963

27″ x 36″   *South Australian Brewing Company Limited*

THE NUMBAKULLA AND THE FIRST ABORIGINES

The myths of the central Australian Aranda tribe describing the creation of the first aborigines differ markedly from those of other Australian peoples.

The Aranda myth tells how, at one time in the dim and ghostly past, two great beings called the Numbakulla brothers, who lived in the western sky, saw a number of embryonic creatures, the Inapatua, whom it was the duty of those two creators to make into aboriginal men and women.

These Inapatua were crouched under low boulders on the shores of the salt lakes; the outlines of the different parts of their bodies could be vaguely seen in the rounded masses of which their forms consisted. They had no powers of sight or hearing, or even of movement.

Coming to earth with their stone knives, the Numbakulla took the incomplete bodies of the Inapatua, and began to make them into human beings. Using their knives, they first released the arms and legs of each body; then, by making four cuts at the end of the extremities, made the fingers and toes. The newly created people could now stand upright. With knives, the Numbakulla opened the eyes and the mouth of each one, and with their fingers formed the nose and the ears. The Inapatua then became fully developed men and women.

Gradually these newly formed people increased in numbers and spread over the land, gathering their food and obeying the complex laws of tribal behaviour that belong only to the men and women of the Aranda tribe.

24″ x 36″   *Mrs H. C. McDonald*

THE FROGS AND THE
SOUND OF WIND

One afternoon during the Dreamtime the frogs were
cooking their evening meal when they saw the grass moving
slightly beside them, felt a gentle breeze, and heard a voice
asking for food and for permission to sleep beside the fire
that night.

The frogs, nervous because they could feel but not see the
unknown presence, reluctantly agreed to the request. That
night the frogs slept but little, afraid that their mysterious,
invisible guest might harm them. But with the rising of the
sun they saw the grass moving as their guest departed, and
heard a voice saying: "I'll see you again before long!"

All that day the frogs were too fearful to prepare any food,
nor did the hours of darkness bring them any rest as they
speculated about this new danger.

The next day the frogs were seated on the branches of a
tree on the edge of the river waiting to see the owner of the
mysterious voice. It was almost midday before they saw a
huge whirlwind coming across the plain towards them,
bending the trees and the rushes in its violence.

Suddenly the whirlwind reached the camp of the frogs,
smashing the flimsy shelters into many pieces, and scattering
the fire in all directions. Although the frogs heard a voice
from the middle of the whirling column of dust endeavour-
ing to calm their fears, they dared not wait for the message,
but plunged into the water for safety until the wind had
passed.

This experience gave the frogs such a fright that even
today the slightest movement of wind in the reeds of their
waterhole is enough to make them leap into the security of
the water.

27″ x 36″   *Mr A. E. Stacy*

MANGOWA AND THE
ROUND LAKES

Mangowa, the hunter, waiting silently on the edge of the lake to spear some fish, saw a young and beautiful girl, Pirili, paddling her shallow bark canoe toward the distant shore.

The sight of the graceful body of Pirili, and the ease with which she propelled her simple craft, filled Mangowa with an overwhelming desire to possess her. But, although the old men of the tribe agreed that Mangowa could have Pirili as his wife, she refused to agree to the marriage.

To court her favours, Mangowa brought her the best fish he had speared, but she allowed them to rot in the sun; he gave her scarlet feathers for her hair, and the softest of opossum-skin cloaks, but still she remained adamant to his wooing. Overwhelmed with desire, Mangowa pursued Pirili wherever she went, pleading his cause and protesting his affection until one day, in desperation, he seized the girl and carried her to his camp. Pirili, frantic with terror, tore herself from his arms and, flying into the sky, asked the women of the Milky Way to protect her from Mangowa's unwelcome attentions. Furious that the girl had escaped him, Mangowa followed her and, tearing great handfuls of stars from the Milky Way, threw them at Pirili to drive her back to earth.

But the people of the stars, disgusted over Mangowa's behaviour, banished him to earth, so that Pirili would always be safe in the sparkling constellation of the Seven Sisters. And the stars that Mangowa tore from their homes, falling to earth, made the circular lagoons that fringe the shores of the coastal lakes of South Australia.

27" x 36"   *Mr K. H. Kingsley*

INUA'S LADDER

An old Opossum-man, Kapili, his wives, two Crow-women, and their brother, Inua, lived on the sea-coast of Arnhem Land. One day, after Kapili had quarrelled with his wives over food, the old man embarked in his canoe and paddled to a distant island to visit some friends.

Meanwhile the brother and his sisters, desiring a change of diet from the fruits of the jungle, built a trap at the mouth of a near-by river, in which the family caught so many fish that when they had eaten them, the ground around their camp was littered with the discarded backbones.

After some days, Kapili returned, and ordered his wives to bring him some food. They angrily refused, telling him that if he wanted food he had better get it for himself. The old man, too exhausted after his long canoe journey to hunt, sat down by the fire to warm himself, and fell asleep.

Seeing this, the woman took a wooden dish, scooped up the hot coals and burning wood from their fire, and poured them over the naked body of their husband. Screaming with pain, Kapili rushed into the sea to ease his suffering, while his wives, knowing he would take vengeance on them, fled into the jungle.

Hearing the commotion and cries of pain in the camp, and not wishing to be involved in a domestic quarrel, Inua, making a ladder from the backbones of the fish lying on the ground, climbed into the sky. But when he heard that Kapili had killed his sisters for their cruelty, Inua descended to earth again, and took their bodies back with him into the sky, where the whole family were changed into stars.

Since those days, the Crow-women and their brother have always lived in the sky. Every day they collect their food from the Milky Way, every night they sit quietly among the stars, safe from the vengeance of Kapili, the bad-tempered Opossum-man.

Inns's Ladder.

Andrew Roberts
1965

36″ x 27″   Mrs Malcolm Brooks

THE SEVEN EMU SISTERS

Wanjin, the men of the Dingo totem, desired as their wives the seven Emu sisters, the Makara. But the unwilling women evaded their suitors by flying to another locality, for in those remote times emus had full-sized wings.

To escape the advances of the Wanjin, the Makara sisters made their home under the tumbled boulders of a rocky outcrop, but the Dingo-men, with their keen sense of smell, soon found out where the women were hiding.

Realizing that they could not lure the women from their home, the Dingo-men lit a bushfire that quickly surrounded the whole outcrop. The men knew that the smoke would drive the Makara into the open, and that the blazing fire would so scorch the wings of the Makara that they could be easily captured.

The plans of the Wanjin were only partly successful; the flames from the bushfire did deprive the Emu-women of the power of flight, but the strenuous efforts of the Makara to step over the burning grass and bushes made their legs grow so long that even to this day the Emu can outdistance almost every other creature.

Escaping from the fire, the Makara ran to the ends of the earth, but still the Wanjin followed them. Finally the desperate women rose up into the sky to become the group of stars known today as the Seven Sisters. The Wanjin men, so that they could still pursue the Seven Sisters, also went into the sky, changing themselves to the constellation of Orion. But the Emu-women are always the first to reach the western horizon, where, for a time, they are safe from the unwelcome attentions of the Dingo-men.

26″ x 33″   *Mrs T. B. Simpson*   57

THE LIGHTNING-MAN
WALA-UNDAYUA

The aborigines of northern Arnhem Land are afraid of the mythical Lightning-man, Wala-undayua. During the dry season he spends most of his time in a deep waterhole in the Liverpool River, though sometimes he hunts for wallabies among the cabbage palms that grow along its banks.

Wala-undayua looks on these palms as his personal property, and should anyone so much as touch their trunks, he would kill them with a lightning flash. But should an aboriginal throw a stone into his waterhole, an even greater misfortune would happen, for then the Lightning-man, furious over this indignity, would rise into the air and create thunderstorms of such violence that everyone would be destroyed.

But it is when the monsoon rains begin that the Lightning-man becomes most belligerent. Leaving his waterhole, he travels in the clouds, roars with the voice of thunder, and with his long arms and legs (which are the lightning flashes) savagely strikes the ground, leaving the burnt-out forest and shattered trees of the devastated landscape as evidence of his wrath.

At the end of the wet-season, Wala-undayua returns to his waterhole, where he lives peacefully until the monsoon clouds again form in the sky to renew his violence.

28″ x 36″   *Mrs C. Lindsay Mills*

THE WOMA SNAKE-MAN

Two groups of Snake-people, the Woma and the Kunia, once lived together in the desert country of central Australia. Every day they went out hunting, and every evening they returned to the same camp and cooked the birds and animals they had killed.

But, as time passed, the Kunia Snake-men began to leave the soft sand and warm sunshine of the desert, and to hunt for their food among the boulders of the ranges. So one evening, after a long discussion around their campfire, the Snake-men agreed to separate—the Woma to stay where they were, and the Kunia to make their homes in the rocky places of the hills.

A large family of the Kunia Snake-people settled among the great boulders on the eastern and southern sides of Ayers Rock, where they lived contentedly, gathering their food among the rocks, and their water from the near-by springs. But one day a party of the venomous Liru Snake-people came from the west, and attacked and killed all the harmless Kunia. Today, the bodies of those Snake-people, and the camps in which they once lived, have been transformed into large groups of boulders around the base of Ayers Rock.

Then came a time when one of the Woma Snake-men of the sandhill country set out on a journey to Ayers Rock. But when he saw, from a distance, that his friends the Kunia had all been killed, he was so overcome with grief that he transformed himself into a snake, which lives only in the red sandhills of the central Australian deserts.

The Mora

Namble Roberts
1957

24″ x 36″   *Mr T. G. H. Strehlow*

WULUWAIT THE BOATMAN
OF THE DEAD

When the long mourning rituals of the aborigines of
Arnhem Land are completed, and the bones of the dead
person are at last interred in the log coffin, his spirit or the
Mokoi, as it is called, leaves his place of burial, and entering
a bark canoe, is paddled by the ghostly boat-man,
Wuluwait, to the island of Purelko, the aboriginal "heaven."

The journey takes many days, for Purelko lies far beyond
the rising of the sun and the morning star: during the
journey many dolphins swim beside the canoe to guide it to
its destination.

When the canoe nears the shores of Purelko, a masked
plover, who has been watching the progress of the canoe,
rises into the air with a shrill call to tell the spirits that
Wuluwait and his companion, the Mokoi, have arrived.

The leader of the aboriginal heaven welcomes the new
spirit, but before he can take any part in the community life
of Purelko, the Mokoi must submit to an ordeal in which the
men of Purelko cast spears into his body until his skin
becomes hard, and impervious to wounds. This ordeal
transforms the new spirit into a young healthy person of
cheerful temperament, for, in Purelko there must be
universal happiness and goodwill.

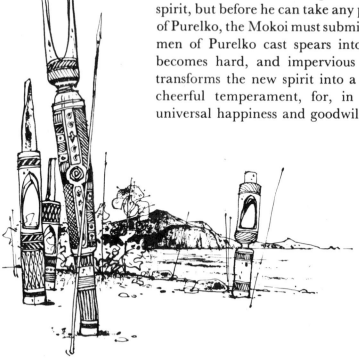

Walmar . . . Boatmen of the Dead

Amélie Robertson
1959

MIRRAM AND WAREEN
THE HUNTERS

In the long distant Dreamtime, Mirram and Wareen were
mighty hunters and the closest of friends. But although they
roamed the country together and shared the food they
caught, they had their likes and dislikes, just as men have
today.

At night, Wareen liked a roof over his head, and always
made a shelter for himself, but Mirram preferred the
freedom of the open spaces and camped under the stars.

All went well until one night a sudden downpour of rain
put out Mirram's fire. Cold, wet, and feeling sorry for himself, he thought how warm and dry Wareen must be. As the
rain grew heavier and the wind bent the trees and bushes,
Mirram ran to Wareen for shelter until the storm had
passed. But Wareen was in a bad mood and told Mirram
that he was not going to share his comfort with someone
who was too lazy to build a shelter of his own.

Surprised, and then enraged at his friend's harsh attitude,
Mirram picked up a large stone and threw it at Wareen. It
hit him on the head, crushing his forehead quite flat.
Roaring with pain, Wareen hurled a spear, which lodged
deep in Mirram's spine.

Wareen, with his flattened forehead, changed into the
Wombat, forever destined to live in a deep, dark hole.
Mirram, with Wareen's spear now grown into a long thick
tail, became the Kangaroo, who still follows his ancestor's
love for the open plains.

These two creatures are still unfriendly, and do their best
to avoid each other.

27" x 36"   *Mr L. M. Goode*   65

THE CREATION OF THE EAGLE AND THE CROW

Mulyan, an Eagle-man, whose camp was on the banks of the River Murray, once married a beautiful girl of the Crow tribe, who bore him a son of whom he was very proud. But one day he saw his wife talking to a Magpie-man whose behaviour was not above suspicion and, being a jealous man, Mulyan punished his wife so severely that she died.

When Wahn, the Crow-man, heard that Mulyan had killed his sister, he was furious, and plotted to avenge her death. But, knowing that the Eagle-man was both powerful and clever, he decided to act by guile rather than by force. So he waited until his nephew was a well-grown child before he sought revenge.

One day, Wahn arrived at the Eagle-man's camp, foot-sore and weary, and asked to be allowed to rest for a while, a request that was readily granted. But, when Mulyan had gone out hunting, the Crow-man speared Mulyan's son. Then, by trampling down the bushes, he made it appear that several men had taken part in the killing. Later, Wahn told the Eagle-man how a number of men had attacked the camp without warning, and killed his son before they disappeared.

Although the keen eye of the Eagle-man recognized that all the tracks belonged to the Crow-man, he gave no sign that he had detected the lie, but sorrowfully asked the Crow-man if he would dig a deep grave for the dead child.

When the grave was dug, and Wahn was at the bottom of it, arranging the dead body, the Eagle-man pushed all the earth into the grave and stamped it down. Then he returned to his camp, certain that he had killed the Crow-man. But Mulyan was mistaken, for the Crow-man, using his magic, had escaped, and called up a heavy thunderstorm that increased in violence until a great flash of lightning struck the camp of the Eagle-man, scattering its fragments everywhere.

Just as Wahn was rejoicing at the success of his revenge, he saw Mulyan rise into the sky and fly away in the form of the eagle-hawk. Nor did the Crow-man escape, for the lightning-flash had so scorched his feathers that even today all crows are as black as night.

Crucifixion of the Eagle

36" x 28"   *Mr and Mrs M. A. Klemich*

THE FROG-WOMAN, QUORK-QUORK, AND HER FAMILY

An aboriginal myth from northern Australia tells of the green frog, Quork-Quork, and her three children—Bumerali, the Lightning-woman; Pakadringa, the Thunder-man; and Tomituka, the Woman of the Monsoon Rains.

No aboriginal will kill or even injure a green frog, knowing that, if he did so, Bumerali, the Lightning-woman, would destroy him instantly with her thunderbolt, while the storms made by Pakadringa and Tomituka would flood the countryside and drown many people.

During the wet season, the Lightning-woman, the Thunder-man, and the Woman of the Monsoon Rains travel across the sky in the clouds, while their mother, Quork-Quork, hops from place to place on the sodden ground beneath.

The Frog-woman, proud of the work of her children, croaks with joy when she hears the rain falling in torrents, the thunderstorms raging, and the lightning breaking the trees into many pieces. But when the wet season has ended and the clouds are no longer in the sky, the children of Quork-Quork live in Tuniruna, a land high above the stars and the Milky Way, while Quork-Quork rests peacefully in the damp crevices of the rocks or in the hollow trees until she again hears the sound of falling rain and the clamour of her children in the sky.

21″ x 30″   *Mrs B. C. Prevost*   69

THE MOPADITIS AND THE
BLACK COCKATOOS

The fear of the spirits of the dead, and the desire of the living to please them, form the bases of many aboriginal myths and complicated burial ceremonies.

The people of Melville Island believe that the spirits of the dead, the Mopaditis, live in self-contained communities. They resemble the aboriginal in appearance except that their bodies, having no substance, are only nebulous images of their former selves. No living person has ever seen a Mopaditi, for they are invisible by day, white in the moonlight, and black in the darkness.

The spirit of a newly dead person stays near the grave until the completion of the burial rituals. It then sets out on a long flight to its future home, accompanied by a flock of screaming black cockatoos, who warn the dwellers of the aboriginal "heaven" that a new spirit is on its way.

No matter what its previous state, the Mopaditi is transformed into a young person of good health and equable temperament, for in its new home everyone must be healthy, happy, and at peace with one another.

Normally, these spirits remain in their eternal home, but, now and again, parties of the more recent arrivals return to their previous camping place and watch the burial rites of one of their old friends.

When the ceremonies are over, and the aborigines are asleep, the spirit people repeat the rituals, performing the same dances and chanting the same songs until the glow of the Sun-woman in the eastern sky warns them to hasten back to their new home.

27″ x 33″   *Lieut-Colonel C. P. Dawnay*

THE TRANSFORMATION
OF PARABRUMA

Long ago, on the Northern coast of Australia, there once lived two young men, Yurumu and Mudati, and a young woman, Parabruma.

Mudati and Parabruma were very fond of each other, a fact that infuriated Yurumu, who wanted Parabruma for his wife.

One day, Yurumu saw a bandicoot run for shelter from his grass nest to a hollow tree, and this suggested to him a scheme by which he could get rid of his rival. Sharpening a number of short sticks, he buried them point upward in the middle of the bandicoot's nest, carefully rearranging the dried grass so that the sticks could not be seen. Then, going to Mudati, Yurumu persuaded him to go hunting.

Eventually, Yurumu led his rival to the faked nest where, pretending excitement, he urged his companion to jump on the nest before the bandicoot escaped. Not suspecting treachery, Mudati did so, forcing the sharp sticks through the soles of his feet. The unfortunate Mudati collapsed on the ground in agony; then, changing himself into a fork-tailed kite, rose into the air and flew away.

Yurumu, overjoyed with his success, quickly sought out the woman Parabruma and proposed marriage. But she, having seen his treachery towards Mudati, angrily refused. Furious over this rebuff, Yurumu picked up his club and hit Parabruma on the head till long pieces of bleeding skin hung down on either side of her face. Screaming with pain (the call of the bird today), Parabruma transformed herself into the masked plover, whose red flaps of skin still hang down on each side of her face.

The Transformation of Tiresias

28″ x 38″   *Mr & Mrs Harry S. Hanks*

73

ULAMINA AND THE STOLEN CANOE

Lying off the northern coasts of Australia was an island, rich in fruit and game, which the Bandicoot-men could not visit because the only canoe in the country was owned by a selfish Star-fish man, Ulamina, who refused to lend it to anyone.

One Bandicoot-man, Banguruk, who was determined to steal the canoe, set out to make friends with the Star-fish man. If Ulamina needed help, Banguruk was always ready to assist, and should the Bandicoot-man spear a kangaroo, he always gave half to the Star-fish man, until the latter began to trust him.

One day, Banguruk was overjoyed to receive an invitation from Ulamina to go out in his canoe on a turtle-hunt. The Bandicoot-man caught a large turtle, and, being much stronger than his companion, pulled the canoe up on the beach, put the turtle on his shoulder, and carried it over the ridge of the sandhill, out of sight of the sea and the canoe.

When the other Bandicoot-men saw the smoke from the fire on which the turtle was being cooked, they sneaked along the beach, launched the canoe, and paddled out to sea.

After a while, the Star-fish man became suspicious, looked over the sandhill, and saw. the other Bandicoot-men paddling his canoe to the distant island.

Ulamina rushed into the sea after his canoe, but, realizing that he was outwitted, he changed himself into a star-fish, and made his home on the sea-bottom. Even to this day, he waves his arms about, hoping one day to recapture the canoe stolen from him by the Bandicoot-men.

25″ x 33″   *Mrs John Gebhardt*

THE NATIVE CAT, THE OWL, AND THE EAGLE

The mythical people of the aborigines' Dreamtime were both evil and good, just as men are today. Of all the evil people, the Native-cat man, Kinigar, was most feared, for he killed for the sheer joy of taking life.

When Kinigar was about, the women and children stayed in their camps, while the men, if forced to travel, always carried their spears and spearthrowers. Yet in spite of these precautions the haunts of the Native-cat man were strewn with the lifeless bodies of men, women, and children.

This slaughter became so serious that the tribal elders agreed that, at all costs, Kinigar must die. After rejecting many schemes, the men decided to block the openings of all springs but one; thus forcing Kinigar to drink at the remaining water-hole, where the best spear-men would be hidden.

The Owl-man, Mopoke, and the Eagle-man, Wildu, who had been chosen for this task, went to the spring before dawn and prepared an ambush. Here they waited patiently throughout a long hot day until, in the late afternoon, they heard Kinigar coming. The Native-cat man, after carefully searching the surrounding bush to make sure there were no enemies about, had just bent down to drink when the waiting men speared him in so many places that he died.

That evening the aborigines saw a red star rise slowly into the sky from the spring where the Native-cat man had been killed. A few days later an unknown cat-like creature, covered with white spots, was seen running about in the grass.

The red star of Betelgeus in the constellation of Orion is the spirit of Kinigar: the little creature that still lives in the bush is his transformed body, the white spots on his coat being the scars from the spear wounds that killed him.

27″ x 36″   *Mr Robert H. Irwin*

THE BAILER-SHELLS,
THE DOLPHINS, AND
THE TIGER-SHARK

The natural features of some of the small islands off the coasts of the Gulf of Carpentaria—the stony outcrops, the steep cliffs, the submerged rocks—were created in the distant past by three groups of mythical people: they were the Bailer-shells, Yukana; the Dolphins, Amatuana; and the Tiger-shark, Bangudja.

A family of the Bailer-shell people made their first camp, now a low rocky hill, on the shores of Bickerton Island, but later moved northwards to Chasm Island. Here they became friendly with a pair of dolphins, with whom they lived happily for a long time, gathering the abundant sea foods, and playing together in the warm waters.

But one day the Tiger-shark, Bangudja, always bent on murder, came into the waters of Chasm Island. He attacked the peaceful community and, after a long chase and a violent struggle, killed the Dolphin-man. This unjustified attack so terrified the Dolphin-woman and her Bailer-shell friends that they fled to a neighbouring island, where the woman changed herself into a long boulder on the sea-coast, and the Bailer-shell family became a spectacular column at the summit of the island.

On the face of a cliff at Chasm Island, Bangudja is now a large red stain that bears a strong resemblance to a tiger-shark, and the body of the murdered Dolphin-man is a rock, awash at low tide.

32" x 26"   *Mr C. Ronald Aitken*